Processing the Pandemic

---

19 days of simple self-reflection to help reset your mindset from COVID19

Copyright

Title book: Processing the Pandemic

Author book: Sarah Blackburn, LMHC

Dedicated to ...

This self-help book is dedicated to anyone who experienced
the COVID19 Pandemic.

Table of contents

<u>Preface</u>

What a ride, huh? Experiencing a pandemic most of us probably thought we would not see in our lifetimes. Everything from social distancing, wearing masks, fear of becoming ill and everything else in between. No matter what side you land on regarding politics, the pandemic was a shared experience that impacted everyone one way or another. Let me tell you... it was a hell of a time to be a mental health counselor as well. Not only were my colleagues and I trying to help others stay afloat- we were also trying to keep ourselves and our families up too. This 19-day bounce back was designed to help you reflect on the past two years of the pandemic, process through what you have experienced, and be able to move forward.

A special shout out to all my colleagues in the helping professions that gave most of themselves to help others during this time. The true heroes in my eyes.

<u>Chapter 1</u>

<u>Day One – The Magic Questions</u>

Imagaine that you are fast asleep, laying in your comfortable bed. You awaken to the sun shining on your face, the smell of coffee brewing, and you notice that all your concerns that accumulated during the last few years of the pandemic are completely gone.

How do you first notice that your concerns are gone?

How does your body feel now that your concerns are gone?

What does your life look like now that your concerns are gone?

These are all reflective questions that we must ask ourselves in order to gain perspective on what has *really* impacted us over the last few years.

Take today to enjoy a sip or two of that coffee and use the following page to write down your thoughts. It could be pictures, words or phrases.

<u>Chapter 2</u>

<u>Day Two – Spheres of Influence</u>

By now, you've more than likely heard about how there are things within your control, and things outside of your control. During the pandemic, there were many times that we, as a community, were left with uncertainty. This uncertainty and the feeling of a "loss of control" impacted our mental health significantly as a collective. Everything from grocery shopping to seeing family became a stragetic maneouver as we attempted to navigate what was best for ourselves, while respecting what others' thought was best for them.

Take today to write down the concerns that you had during the pandemic that were inside of your control and outside your control.

Pro Tip: If you need help, think about yesterday and the different things that you felt were "magically gone" in your perfect scenario.

<u>Chapter 3</u>

<u>Day Three – Shifting Focus</u>

Research has shown that when we shift our focus to what we can control, we are able to see meaningful lasting differences in our mental health, physical health and overall well-being.

Reflect on your responses to yesterday's prompt on spheres of influence. Which **three** things that you wrote down in the area of things you *can control* have impacted your overall mental health the most during the pandemic? The focus will be on these areas as we progress through the following 16 days.

1. ____

2. ____

3. ____

Chapter 4

<u>Day four – Grounding</u>

There is something to be said for interventions that help us get into a better frame of mind in order to tackle the challenging days. This technique is called a *Grounding Exercise* is designed to focus on the senses and thus break the cycle of rumination and negative thought patterns. You can do this technique at just about any time, in just about any place.

As soon as you notice your thoughts starting to build up...
- Find <u>5</u> things that you can see
- <u>4</u> things you can hear
- Pick <u>3</u> things you can smell
- <u>2</u> things you can touch
- And <u>1</u> thing you can taste

As you do this, really investigate each object that you see/hear/smell/touch/taste. For this to be fully effective, you must be in the moment and mindful of when the intrusive thoughts come back. If they do, refocus to whatever object you are working on and continue the exercise.

Pro tip: Practice this when you are in a calm state so that you can get a good feel for the intervention. When you start to have a more challenging time, you will already know how to navigate this exercise.

Chapter 5

<u>Day Five – Anger</u>

Anger is one emotion that came up quite frequently when talking to those that have experienced the pandemic. Anger triggers behavior, emotion, physiological and cognitive response systems. These systems co-occur during an anger response and rapidly reinforce each other – which makes it that much more difficult to control!

Consider when you identified the things you could control, and the things you could not. Did doing this illicit any anger responses within you? If it did, you are not alone.

Ron Potter-Efron is considered an expert in the field of anger management. He identifies various type of anger that manifest which include: survivor anger, impotent anger, attachment anger, and shame anger.

Did you fear that the virus would attack your body and your emotions were expressed in anger (survivor anger)? Where their times when you felt that you would get sick and felt impossibly helpless in the situation, so you experienced anger (impotent anger)? Did you experience times where you felt rejected by your family, friends or those you care about due to their differing belief systems on the pandemic (attachment anger)? Where their times during the pandemic where you felt that you were functioning at a much lower level or had a loss of identity and you felt angry or more irritable due to this (shame anger)? Are you able to identify any times during the pandemic where you were not living up to your morals or values and became angry because of this (shame anger again)?

All of these were normal anger responses due to the body releasing two chemicals in your brain (adrenaline and cortisol) that are geared up to defend yourself against the feeling of being "less than." Most people perceive that they go into an autopilot state of mind and are not able to rationally address situations they are facing. This often leads to overwhelming emotions, not being able to process the situation properly, and building up of stress that can cause many to have other physical symptoms.

Today, reflect on what you now know about anger responses and ask yourself if you identify with any discussed here in this chapter. If so, gaining insight so you can recognize them is the first step in beginning to heal.

<u>Chapter 6</u>

<u>Day Six – Stress Inoculation Therapy (part one)</u>

Stress inocu-what? Have no fear as I'm here to break down this particular concept of therapy that is very helpful in addressing stressful situations. In Stress Inoculation Therapy (SIT) the goal is to help clients becomes educated about stressful situations, the universal nature of stress, and the undesirable outcomes they may be vulnerable to experiencing when they are confronted with the stressful situation. The hope is to give you a better understanding of this concept so that you can anticipate how to address future stressful events now that you've made it though this major life event.

The first thing that I want you to take a look at is how much you know about the universal nature of stress. Take some time to do some light research looking further into the root of what causes stress in your brain. Next, look into adressing the potential threat. If you reflect on the pandemic, were these aspects that caused you to become more stressed than others? Do you feel that you were appropriately equiped to handle these aspects as they arose? If you answered no to the last question, you may need to look at developing additional coping skills to assist you next time a stressor like that occurs.

Continue to reflect on the difference between the aspects of your stressors and the stress-induced reactions that you have. Are their areas that you just won't be able to change when it comes to your stressors. This is important to know when you move forward to the next chapter.

Pro tip: If this chapter causes a need to process more than one day, that is *more* than okay. Everyone takes in information differently and this book is no different. Praise yourself for recongizing that you needed that extra time!

Chapter 7

<u>Day Seven – Stress Inoculation Therapy (part two)</u>

Skills, skills, skills... that is what this chapter is all about. Developing the various skills to address stress is vital in your stress management and overall well-being. The most effective types of skills to build are those of emotion regulation, socialization, communication, problem-solving and relaxation. It is important to be mindful that what works for your neighbor, friend or colleague may not work for you. Each person is unique and understanding and developing your skills tailored to your needs is paramount.

How to socialize, communicate, relax and problem-solve effectively are all avenues that we will explore in later chapters. For now, I want to pay closer attention to emotional regulation. Below is a method to help with emotional regulation that has been proven effective when it comes to psychology intervention research.

<u>Adaptive Coping with Emotions (ACE) Method</u>

This model focuses on awareness of your affective states; being able to identify and label the affective states; understanding the affective states and if the emotion can be changed or not; modification of the affective states; acceptance of the affective states and tolerating what you will not be able to change; being ready to confront situations that may cue the negative affective state; and being able to effectively self-support when faced with the challenges.

 **Pro tip**: Affective state is the biological and psychological state that you are in as you attempt to cope with your environment.

\

Chapter 8

<u>Day Eight – Stress Inoculation Therapy (part three)</u>

Finally, you made it to the final day of processing how to assist with helping yourself in stressful situations. In the final part of SIT, you look at applying the information you have learned and follow through. As the saying goes, Rome wasn't built in a day!

Take time today to reflect on the knowledge you know about stress now, strategies you have for managing stress, and plans to keep it under control (the best you can) as these situations arise in the future.

Pro tip: Simulation methods help to increase the sense of "realism" as you practice your skills. Some of these methods include visualization, vicarious learning, role playing, modeling and repetition.

Chapter 9

Day Nine – The big Three

Back on day three, you reflected on three things that you *are* able to control. Process through if you have gained insight into these situations using what you know now about your anger response and stress inoculation therapy.

Document that here:

____

____

____

____

____

____

____

____

____

____

<u>Chapter 10</u>

<u>Day Ten – Communication & DBT</u>

How much did our communication change during the pandemic? From school going virtual, video conferences over computers, drive by birthday parties and so much more. We had to adapt to this new, uncomfortable environment that we were now expected to live in.

Healthy and stable relationships of any kind can be a tremendous source of positive emotions, connection and overall support. Dialectical Behavioral Therapy (DBT) addresses communication skills in the Interpersonal Effectiveness module. The four main areas it identifies in regard to communication are:

Assertive: You can express your emotions, needs and thoughts clear and honest to others. You are aware of both your needs as well as the needs of others.

Passive: You tend to avoid expressing emotions and attempt to block your thoughts and emotions alike. At times, you loom in doubt and worry about triggering bad feelings or conflict.

Aggressive: You tend to care more about meeting your own personal needs/goals than that of others. At times, you can become verbally aggressive when communicating and feel the need to control the situation

Passive-aggressive: You tend to express your emotions in indirect ways. It can become unclear to the other person what you are trying to convey. You may use the silent treatment or sarcasm often in your communication which leaves others confused.

Is there a style that you feel you fit in with the most? Once you can identify this type, reflect on these three questions:

1. Who do I generally use this communication style with?
2. What is the level of effectiveness with this communication style?
3. How does using this communication style impact me?

Understanding communication improves your overall interpersonal effectiveness and well-being. This will assist in giving you more insight *and* a better perspective when addressing situations. Hopefully there isn't another pandemic in our lifetime where communication transforms so quickly but understanding these communication styles is very important as we continue to navigate those changes.

Chapter 11

Day Eleven – Take Five

You might have heard about various relaxation techniques from everyone from doctors to yoga instructors. During the pandemic, it was especially important to take a few moments to keep relaxing yourself and practice a calmer state of mind. This allows you to be able to address what you need to with clarity. Having a few effective relaxation techniques in your toolbox is very important to grounding yourself and creating a safe space to process life's events as well.

Today, I want you to reflect on the relaxation skills that you have developed over time. Pick one, dust it off, and take it for a spin. How did it feel to take those few moments to calm your mind?

Here are some of my favorite relaxation techniques for you to try:

- Autogenic relaxation

- Progressive muscle relaxation

- Visualization

- Music & art

- Hydrotherapy

- Massage

Pro tip: Try these relaxation skills on a schedule for a week. Note how you feel in the beginning of the week, and how you feel at the end. Assess the effectiveness of the skill(s) you tried and how you might be able to tweak it to better fit your lifestyle and needs.

Chapter 12

Day Twelve – Social Butterfly

Another way the pandemic shaped us these past years is when it comes to socialization. Families spend the holidays away from each other. Funerals went on without friends and loved ones being able to say goodbye. High School and college graduations… stopped. Humans are social beings, and this dysregulated many of us down to our core. For some, the only faces they saw were over a computer screen for months or even years at a time. With this, many people began to develop symptoms of depression and anxiety. Small tasks now became stressful and interacting with strangers now became worrisome.

Today, I want you to simply make a commitment to get back in touch with those you care about. Anything from a cup of coffee at the park, to a night out creating art… just anything to reconnect with others.

My idea for getting back in touch:

____

____

<u>Chapter 13</u>

<u>Day Thirteen – Let's talk about vagus!</u>

The vagus nerve. This nerve is more important than you may realize! It is the longest nerve in the body which starts in the brain, travels down the neck, passes around the digestive system, liver, heart, lungs, pancreas and spleen. It is a huge part of the parasympathetic nervous system as well.

Now we are going to dive into science a bit, so bear with me! "Vagal tone" is a body function that is measured by your tracking your breathing rate with your heart rate. When you breathe in, your heart rate speeds up a bit and then slows down again when you breathe out. The *larger* the difference between your heart rate when you inhale and your heart rate when you exhale means that you have a <u>higher vagal tone</u>. What does this mean to have a "high vagal tone?" A higher tone is associated with your body being able to relax faster after encountering stress.

So, now the big question is how can you increase your vagal tone? Research has suggested that slow, deep, rhythmic breathing is a great way to increase your vagal tone. Additional skills include humming, speaking, washing your face with cold water and meditation. These practices have shown to improve everything from depression and stress to high blood pressure and digestive upsets.

Today, try one of these exercises.
Reflect on how you feel afterwards.

Chapter 14

Day Fourteen – Cognitive Distortions

On day fourteen, let's look at one of the foundational concepts of CBT therapy: Cognitive Distortions. There are many lists floating around of the various types of cognitive distortions that have been researched. For simplicity's sake, I will introduce you to the ten.

All of nothing thinking: You have a habit of looking at things in black and white. "All or nothing." For you, there is no gray area.

Labeling: You identify with something you believe is a shortcoming. When you make a mistake, you would normally tell yourself you're a "loser" rather than positive self-talk that you only made a mistake.

Blame/Personalization: You often find yourself blaming yourself for something you were not 100% responsibly for. On the other side, you may only blame others for the problem and not look at how your attitude or behaviors could have influenced the situation.

Jumping to Conclusions: You might find yourself thinking that you are "mind reading" or assuming that people are reacting negatively to you when there is no solid evidence. You also may "fortune tell" or arbitrarily predict things that will turn out for the worse.

Overgeneralization: You tend to view events as negative and create a pattern of feeling defeated.

"Should" Statements: You often find yourself criticizing yourself or others with "should", "shouldn'ts" "oughts," "musts" or anything in that ballpark.

Discounting the Positives: You may push your positive qualities and accomplishments to the side in favor of a negative perspective.

Mental Filter: You tend to overthink and dwell on the negatives and ignore all the other positives that are happening.

Magnification/Minimization: You find yourself blowing things out of proportion or shrink their importance down. Either are disproportionate.

Emotional Reasoning: You tend to find yourself making your emotions fact. For example, "I feel like I made a dumb decision so I must in fact be stupid."

Most people experience distortions throughout their life based on the circumstances they encounter. It is not a sign of mental illness necessarily, but it does point towards a negative lens in which you tend to process situations, conversations and potentially, life.

Pro tip: Take a moment to do this mindfulness breathing exercise before answering the questions. That way you give your mind a few moments to absorb the information and answer from a clear mind.

Take a moment to take a deep breath in to the count of four.
Hold your breath for the count of four.
Release your breath for to the count of four.
Keep your breath out for a count of four.

Complete this exercise three times and clear your mind.

Do you identify with any of them?
If so, which ones?
Do you do them with anyone particular?
Do you think the cognitive distortion increased your stress during the pandemic?

Chapter 15

Day Fifteen – Bringing it back

Yup. Going back to day three again and the three things you can change. Were you viewing them using any of the cognitive distortions? Would any of the socialization, communication or skills learn help these three things that you are able to change?

As you reflect, create your plan of action on how to address each item that you have in your control, and wish to change.

Pro tip: SMART goals are one of the best ways to not only track your goal but make it achievable.

S – SPECIFIC

M – MEASUREABLE

A – ACHIEVEABLE

R – RELEVANT

T – TIME BOUND

Document your plan here:

Thing you can change #1:

____

____

S -

____

____

M -

____

____

A -

____

____

R -

____

____

T -

____

____

Thing you can change #2:

____

____

S -

____

____

M -

____

____

A -

____

____

R -

____

____

T -

____

____

Thing you can change #3:

____

____

S -

____

____

M -

____

____

A -

____

____

R -

____

____

T -

____

____

<u>Chapter 16</u>

<u>Day Sixteen – Build your tribe</u>

As we near the end of this nineteen-day process, I want you to look at your support system. Through this pandemic, many of us have learned who is there for us when times get hard- and who is not. Who was the one that brought you that massive toilet paper haul when you were sick at home with the family? Who was the one that cheered you up and tried to reach out during the hard days? Who showed up, checked in and made sure that you were, okay?

Today, build your tribe. Envision those that support you and care for you surrounding and embracing you. Who are those people? Why are they there? What makes them your tribe?

<u>Chapter 17</u>

<u>Day Seventeen – You at your best</u>

Today, let's process through a specific time (recently or in the past) when you felt that you were at your best. Did you handle a tough situation with ease? Were you able to navigate a hardship with grit and perseverance? Pick a time where you felt that you were your most authentic self. When you felt proud, confident and happy. Spend a few moments bringing this time back to the present.

Now, take some time to write down this situation in more concreate terms. Ask yourself the where, when, why, what and how questions to get a better understanding of the situation. Make sure to add in your strengths during this situation as well as was successes you experienced and feelings that you had. How were you able to achieve your goals in this situation?

Pro tip: Grab a highlighter or circle all the strengths that you possessed in this situation. How can you utilize these strengths in daily life?

Write the situation down here.

<u>Chapter 18</u>

<u>Day Eighteen – Radical Acceptance</u>

Radical acceptance is a new concept to most. You may have heard about accepting the things you cannot change, but radical acceptance goes deepr than this. It is about accepting life on life's terms and not resisting what you cannot or choose not to change. Radical acceptance is about saying yes to life, **just as it is.**

Whoa. This seems impossible, right? Here are some ways to connect to the concept of radical acceptance to incorporate it into your everyday life.

- Identify the situations in your life that you are having a hard time accepting (see chapter 2)
- Feel and accept the emotions tied to when thinking about stressful events.
- Accept things as they are instead of how you want them, or imagine them, to be.
- Understand what is within your control and outside your control. (See chapter 2).
- Find ways to ground yourself or calm yourself down. (see chapters 4, 11 & 13)
- See yourself as an observer rather than a participant.
- Practice radical acceptance each day to make the habit easier.

- Radical acceptance may be the answer when: you are unable to solve a problem or change your perspective on it.
- Watch your thoughts for signs of not accepting.
- Remind yourself that reality can't be changed (such as the pandemic).
- Be aware of how you are feeling in your body.
- Accept that life can be worthwhile even when experiencing pain or hardship.
- Allow yourself to let go of the need to control situations.
- Allow yourself to be imperfect, we make mistakes!
- Stop judging situations or attaching a value to them (good or bad) (see chapter 14)
- Engage in journaling and self-reflection to understand your emotions.
- Keep notes on when you feel judgmental.
- Look for patterns in your negative thoughts.
- Relax your body and watch how you are breathing (see chapter 13).
- See people as human and not all good or all bad (see chapter 14)
- Forgive yourself but also learn to move on and accept responsibility.
- Be okay with allowing yourself to stop thinking about how things "could have been."(see chapter 14)

.and...

seek out a therapist if you feel you cannot navigate these feelings on your own!

<u>Chapter 19</u>

<u>Day Nineteen – Final Thoughts</u>

These past nineteen days were full of building skills, reflection, introspection and courage. You were able to navigate all of this and hopefully you feel in a better place than you started nearly three weeks ago.

If you feel like continued conversation or therapy would be beneficial, I encourage you to reach out to find a clinician to carry on this process. It's all about **progress**, *not perfection.*

I wish you nothing but the best as you continue your journey to bounce back from the COVID19 pandemic. You got this!

"The secret of change is to focus all of your energy not on fighting the old, but on building the new" -Socrates

References

Biswas-Diener, R. & Dean, B. (2007). Positive Psychology Coaching: Putting the Science of Happiness to Work for Your Clients. Hoboken, NJ: John Wiley & Sons, Inc.

Buruck, G., Dörfel, D., Kugler, J., & Brom, S. S. (2016). Enhancing well-being at work: The role of emotion regulation skills as personal resources. *Journal of Occupational Health Psychology, 21*(4), 480–493. https://doi.org/10.1037/ocp0000023

Chevalier, G. (2015). The effect of grounding the human body on mood [Abstract].
https://www.ncbi.nlm.nih.gov/pubmed/25748085

David, Burns D. *The Feeling Good Handbook.* New York: Plume, 1999. Print.

Deffenbacher, J. L. (2011). Cognitive-behavioral conceptualization and treatment of anger. *Cognitive and Behavioral Practice*, 18, 297-298.

Deffenbacher, J. L., & McKay, M. (2000). *Overcoming situational and general anger: A protocol for the treatment of anger based on relaxation, cognitive restructuring, and coping skills training.* Oakland, CA: New Harbinger

Forsythe P, Bienenstock J, Kunze WA. Vagal pathways for microbiome-brain-gut axis communication. Adv Exp Med Biol. 2014;817:115-33.

Kaur, M., *et al.* (2016). An adapted imaginal exposure approach to traditional methods used within trauma-focused cognitive behavioural therapy, trialled with a veteran population.
https://www.ncbi.nlm.nih.gov/pmc/articles/PMC6130742/

Kok, B, Fredrickson, B, Coffey, K, et al. How Positive Emotions Build Physical Health: Perceived Positive Social Connections Account for the Upward Spiral Between Positive Emotions and Vagal Tone. Psychological Science 2013 24: 1123

Linehan, M., M., (2014). DBT Training Manual. New York, NY: The Guilford Press.

Linehan, M. *Cognitive-Behavioral Therapy of Borderline Personality Disorder*. New York: The Guilford Press, 1993.

Potter-Efron, Ronald, and Potter-Efron, Patricia (1989) *Letting Go of Shame: Understanding How Shame Affects Your Life*, New York, HarperCollins/Hazeldon.

University of Virginia, H., 2018. *Writing S.M.A.R.T. Goals*. University of Virginia.